Emotions, Lightly Toasted

A collection of hushes, hugs and heartbeats.

Anila Paul C

Dedication

For my babies Nile, Zidane & Jordan
who filled my heart with songs
before they even knew words.

Preface

Hi there,

This little book is made of moments—some raw, some imagined, some deeply felt.

It's a collection of thoughts that came to me when I was holding my baby, sitting in silence, or just trying to make sense of a feeling or a thought.

They're not perfect. Just honest.

Within these pages, you might brush against tenderness, restlessness, or the soft ache of longing.

You'll find whispers of hope, the hush of stillness, and the warmth of gratitude tucked into quiet corners.

There's melancholy, a dash of defiance, a swirl of nostalgia, and the sugar-rush of playfulness too

all gently held,

all lightly toasted.

If any of these pieces feel familiar to you, like something you've quietly felt too then I'm really glad we met here.

With warmth,

Anila

Acknowledgements

They say it takes a village turns out, it also takes a lot of coffee, late-night ramblings, patient listeners, and a few gentle pushes. Thank you to everyone who cheered me on, laughed at my bad ideas, and pretended to take me seriously when I needed it most.

For Jestin who may not always get my metaphors, but still hopes the rest of the world will. My steady strength, and the silent investor in all my poetic dreams.

For Anichetan and Geethu chechy who reads my poems with care, cheers me on without fail, and stays by my side, always.

For Jetlin who never missed a chance to mock me, yet never left my side.

For both my Ammas to my mother, for giving your life and light to me.

And to my mother-in-law, who from the very start, became my Amma too.

For both my father and father-in-law, for their silent love throughout.

For my whole family you are the reason behind every step I take.

Thank you for all the love, the sacrifices, and the endless care.

1. A Toast

Clink goes the glass—
to the ones who stayed.
To the noise, the love,
the plans we never made.

To laughter that rose
and circled the air,
and hugs that waited
like home at the stair.

To burnt toast mornings,
to shared cups of tea,
to the chaos we carried
so tenderly.

To joy that didn't shout,
but still filled the room,
and messes that bloomed
into memories too soon.

To the hands that held mine
without being asked,
and the hearts that showed up
when the days felt too fast.

Clink once again—
for the now, for the then.
For all that we are.
And all we've been.
Here's to the ones I call family.

2. Completely, Hopelessly in Love

In love with your milk-sweet breaths,
the little hiccups, the big burps,
and those soft sleepy eyes
My tiny one, I'm right here—
with arms full of warmth
and whispers softer than dreams.
Show me that sweet gummy smile,
and brighten my world.
Let me hold you a little
longer.
Tomorrow, you might already be bigger.

3. The Baby Musketeers

Three spoons, one big bowl—
Zidane dives in first.
Jordan follows, mouth wide open.
Nile?
She waits... then scoops the last bite.

There's a drip on the floor,
a drop on a toe,
and a glob of cream
right on someone's nose.

Next come the popsicles!
Lime for Jordan,
Mango for Zidane,
Nile picks the pink one
and licks in slow circles.

Then there's dancing
sugar-high and loud—
a burp from Jordan,

a hiccup from Nile,
Zidane spins twice and falls on his bum
laughter from everywhere.

When the bowl is finally empty,
their cheeks are full,
their shirts a disaster.
the floor? A sticky map of joy

The memory?
Still sweet on their lips.

4. To my dear boy

How you've grown, my dearest one,
From tiny toes to chasing sun.
Once curled within my quiet arms,
Now bounding up with boyish charms.

At just a glance, you light with glee,
No joy runs deeper than yours for me.
You've grown so tall, so strong, so bright,
Yet still my baby in every light.

My sweetest soul, my gentle grace,
My home is found within your face.
My lovely boy, my morning song,
With you is where my joys belong.

I love you more than stars can show,
In ways you may not fully know.
No matter what, come sun or rain,
My love for you will still remain.

You've made me soft, you've made me true,
You've made me more by loving you.
And if I break, it's not from pain
But from the love that I can't contain.

5. Deliciously Yours

Every taste begins here—
with a base baked from buttery love,
soft, steady, and sure.
Over it, I spread a layer of care,
fold in warmth,
whisk in tenderness,
beat in laughter,
sift in comfort,
stir in hope,
And lace it with lovely dreams.

At the very top,
I crown it all
with a cherry-red kiss
ready to melt into sweetness.

6. Nothing Fancy

How about a kiss, a smile,
A cheeky side-glance full of love?
How about hugs, snuggles,
And a heart full of warmth?

How about a pat on the back,
A clap, a cheer, a happy shout?
How about a cup of tea—
Strong and sweet, just like us?

How about we sit together
And share silly stories?
How about we hold hands
And wander through the park?

How about you hold me close,
just a bit longer,
So, every breath reminds me
where my home is
And maybe, just maybe, if all this happened,

Wouldn't the day feel a little brighter—
This lazy, golden noon?

7. Sweetness of Nothing

Why am I idle, just sitting here still?
Why don't I chase some forgotten thrill?
Why do my hands stay empty,
my days stay slow?
Why don't I have somewhere to rush,
somewhere to go?

The questions rise and fall,
like tides tugging at my mind.
They come quietly,
then crash loud against my heart,
then slip away again,
only to return once more.

The guilt rolls in with them,
soft as a wave that never truly leaves.
It asks why I waste the hours,
why I let the days drift by.

But not every moment must be spun into gold,

not every breath must build a castle,
not every hour must bloom into something grand.

Some hours are meant to float,
like clouds across a blue sky.
Some minutes are meant to be empty,
simple, and quietly kind.

And in that space
I find —
the sweetness of doing nothing.

8. The Pause

It's been two days.
No poem, no lines—
just quiet.
No thoughts at all
just still.

I've looked at clouds,
washed a few cups,
sat by the window,
waited—
but nothing came.

Maybe words are
just out walking.
Maybe they'll come back
with pockets full of
Itty bitty songs.

So I sit here,
not chasing them—

just listening

in case

they hum.

9. Happy cheers!

Oh dear, oh dear,
Lend me your ear!
Start the engine, shift the gear,
Leave behind fear.
Make it a cheer,
Don't drop a tear—
Life's too dear,
So take the wheel and steer.
No time to veer,
Just hold your gear.
The path is wide,
The skies are clear.
With dreams to chase
and love to steer,
Go ride your fate
without a rearview mirror near.

10. Remote-ly Attached

Because sometimes, emotions wear pyjamas and binge-watch Friends

From a flat black screen came stories and light,
A portal of dreams, distractions, and delight.
Dragons and detectives, anchors and ads,
Cooking shows, crime scenes, sitcoms with dads.

We roamed the globe from a sunken couch,
Remote in hand, chips in our pouch.
It cheered us up when life threw lemons,
Though one episode was never enough.

It kept us company, in what we never spoke.
Filled the silence, covered the wall.
Yet we sigh, roll eyes, say it rots the brain,
While still bingeing reruns to stay sane.

So maybe it's time we dropped the blame,

It's just a screen.
We're the game.

11. Wandering Thoughts

These thoughts pour out of my head,
I try to catch them, but they slip.
They slide to my face
And linger there, making me look lost—
Lost in a thought.

I brush them off, puff my cheeks,
And put on a smile.
I try to keep the thoughts inside,
But they sink instead—
Down to the quiet alley of my heart,
Where they flutter, wanting to be free.

They slip to my hands,
Run down my fingers,
Tingling and teasing,
Mocking me with a race I can't win.
They reach my legs,
And I run—faster and faster
Only to lose again.

They tumble away,
Rolling across the floor
Like little marbles lost in a game.

The more I gather,
The more they spill—
Spilling secrets everywhere:
Here, there, all around.

I fix my smile like a patch on a leak
And try again to pick them all.
And when that too fails,
I pick myself up,
Take a deep breath,
And rise again for another go.

12. Left over

I brew my feelings in silence,
steeping them slow and deep,
letting them swirl, letting them grow,
until I pour them out
like filtered tea.

But some things are meant to stay behind
the heavy bits, the stubborn dust,
the pieces too thick to pass through.
They settle at the bottom, unseen,
like old dreams and silent wishes.

Not everything can rise with the steam.
Some feelings are meant to stay,
buried deep,
out of reach.

13. Circles we speak

Not far from home, there is a quiet pond
where I once tossed a handful of stones

sometimes slow, with a gentle hand,
sometimes quick, with a flick of the wrist.

I watched the ripples bloom and spread,
the slow ones moved soft and wide,
barely brushing the edges.
The fast ones surged out bold,
startling the stillness.

Not all ripples fade at once—
some, like words, stay a little longer.

The thoughtful ones ripple gently,
leaving space instead of scars.
The sharp ones cut fast and loud,
echoing long after we're done.

The wise ones sink beneath the noise,
settling deep in hidden depths.
And the tactful ones?
They touch, not tear—
careful,
measured,
and real.

14. 7 Minutes

If I could choose what to remember in my final moments

When my brain stops braining,
I hope you will fill in the blanks .
Remind me of our happiest moments,
our small wins
the times we laughed till we cried,
the ordinary days that meant everything.
I want all of that—
and what we built—
packed in a suitcase bursting with love.
Let that be what stays with me
Because I only get seven minutes
before it all shuts down.

And those seven minutes
They aren't small.
They are all.

15. To the Shore, Always

The waves loved the shore.
Oh, how they longed to stay—
To rest a while, to whisper deep secrets,
To tell her all the tales they carried
From the heart of the ocean.

But time was never kind to them.
They rushed in, breathless and full,
Only to be tugged away too soon,
Their voices trailing, stories left untold.

Still, they returned again and again,
Leaving letters inked in white frothy foam
On the ever-waiting sand.
They scattered seashells as quiet clues
Of all the precious moments they wished to share.

The shore, longing as much as the sea,
Waited with eager eyes.
She listened to every wave

As though it might finally stay.
But the sea always called them back—
Not yet, not now, not today.

Yet the waves keep trying.
They come with hope in every curl,
To stay by the shore, if only for a while.
And if you listen closely
At the hush between tides,
You might hear their tale—
in the murmurs of the wind...

16. Afterwords

After the verse ends,
a hush arrives—
softer than syllables,
more certain than rhyme.

The silence
comes dressed in commas,
pauses that ache
where breath once lived.

A dash lingers—
not quite an end,
not quite a beginning—
just a space to feel what wasn't said.

After the rhyme slips away,
only rhythm remains—
heartbeat-light,
tiptoeing through the blank.

She sits
in the echo of stanzas,
where metaphors lost their shape
and full stops
felt too cruel to place.

The page is no longer speaking.
But still,
she listens.

Because sometimes,
the most honest line
is the one that
comes after words.

17. Between Stations

Whooo! goes the whistle—loud and bold,
Engines rumble, stories unfold.
Red turns green with a mighty blare,
The train rolls out into dusty air.

Windows down, the breeze flies in,
Vendors rush with a cheeky grin.
Some hop on, some wave goodbye,
Some find seats and wonder why.

A child leans out for a better view,
Luggage tumbles—a traveling shoe!
A laugh breaks out, a cup rolls wide,
A comic book flutters up to the sky.

No long halts, just chai-time stops,
A quick stretch, some lemon drops.
Back on track with a rocking sway,
Another curve, we're on our way.

The horn sings loud, the bogies sway,
Night turns to dawn, and dreams give way.
The brakes sigh soft, the wheels slow down—
We roll at last into the town.

A yawn, a smile, the bags in tow—
Just like that, it's time to go.

18. Big Shoes, small feet

"Grow up," they said.
You're not little anymore—
act like it.
Hold it all in.
Think twice.
You can't have your way
its not about you anymore.

So you did.
You grew into boxes,
into roles,
into silence.
You traded wonder for worry,
freedom for fear.
And somewhere in all that becoming,
you forgot her.

The child inside—
she never outgrew
the mud between her toes,

dreams that floated free,
and tears that fell without shame.
She still hums lullabies to your pain
when no one is watching.

She peeks through your tired eyes,
stirs through your stillest hours,
nudges you when you forget
how to be soft.
She's still there—
not gone,
just quiet.

Yes, growing up is hard—
a silent snare in a noisy world.
And maybe,
the way out
was simply learning
to listen within.

19. The Audacity

Sorry that I stood my ground,
Sorry I didn't dumb it down.
Sorry I saw through the noise,
Sorry I made my own choice.

Sorry my confidence shook you up,
Sorry I drank from my own cup.
Sorry for being strong and clear,
Sorry I didn't shrink in fear.

Sorry I walked when I was told to stay,
Sorry I danced in my own way.
Sorry for shining a bit too bright—
for getting it wrong by doing it right.

But here's the truth, served with a smirk:
I'm not "sorry,"
I'm your *plot twist.*

20. Fireworks of Emotions

Pink peeks out with a happy face,
green for thoughts not said out loud.
Red for sparks that come and go,
blue for feelings soft and slow.

And white—the calm that holds it all,
like stars that blink, then softly fall.

21. Somewhere in between

My choices rest
on gentle threads—
not always right,
not always best.
But still, I try.

I'm not at the top,
not the very bottom—
just held in place
by what I am.

The things I know
don't beg to shine,
but now and then,
they leave a sign—
they sound like mine.

I wasn't the loudest love,
or the brightest joy—
but I was there,

in ways that mattered.

Between the hello
and the letting go,
between the laugh
and the lump in my throat—

Not the beginning,
nor the close—
just the pause
the silence knows.
The thought that comes
but goes unseen—
the tender heart
of in-between.